EMPOWERED

WORDS UNSPOKEN

Edited By Debbie Killingworth

First published in Great Britain in 2022 by:

Young Writers
Remus House
Coltsfoot Drive
Peterborough
PE2 9BF
Telephone: 01733 890066
Website: www.youngwriters.co.uk

Printed and bound in the UK by BookPrintingUK
Website: www.bookprintinguk.com
YB0491T

✷ FOREWORD ✷

Since 1991, here at Young Writers we have celebrated the awesome power of creative writing, especially in young adults where it can serve as a vital method of expressing their emotions and views about the world around them. In every poem we see the effort and thought that each student published in this book has put into their work and by creating this anthology we hope to encourage them further with the ultimate goal of sparking a life-long love of writing.

Our latest competition for secondary school students, Empowered, challenged young writers to consider what was important to them. We wanted to give them a voice, the chance to express themselves freely and honestly, something which is so important for these young adults to feel confident and listened to. They could give an opinion, share a memory, consider a dilemma, impart advice or simply write about something they love. There were no restrictions on style or subject so you will find an anthology brimming with a variety of poetic styles and topics. We hope you find it as absorbing as we have.

We encourage young writers to express themselves and address subjects that matter to them, which sometimes means writing about sensitive or contentious topics. If you have been affected by any issues raised in this book, details on where to find help can be found at www.youngwriters.co.uk/info/other/contact-lines

✷ CONTENTS ✷

The Oratory Preparatory School, Goring Heath

Joe Barratt	68
Kiara Kemahli (12)	69
Tom Holborn (12)	70
Emilia Bish (11)	72
Tiger Wang (12)	73
Darcy Pollard (12)	74
Archie White (12)	75
Amelia Cole (13)	76
Freddie Bennett (12)	77
Iris Gray (13)	78
Giorgia Fiorentino (13)	79
Mallory Ross (12)	80
Orla Huxtable (13)	81
Skyla Horton-Moran (12)	82
Lily Bowlby (12)	83
Zubyn Mehta (12)	84
Henry Kietz (12)	85
Jessica Reed (12)	86
Tara Bignell (12)	87
Samantha Wesson (11)	88
Thomas Eady (12)	89
Noah Moore (12)	90
Jasper Vaughan (13)	91
Dylan Wheat (13)	92
Mia Burridge (11)	93
Scarlett Baker (12)	94
Emily Caine (11)	95
Dorcus Hobley (12)	96
Amy Prodhan (11)	97
Freddie Sallis (11)	98
Kitty Thomas (11)	99
Finley South (12)	100
Harry Wakeman (12)	101
Anya Jacobs (12)	102
Finn Mackenzie (12)	103
Ronnie Phares (12)	104
Barnaby Badcock (13)	105
Rosie Davis (12)	106
George Hall (11)	107
Lucas Teixeira (12)	108
Toby Jomar (12)	109

Erin Robertson (11)	110
Freddie Bowlby (11)	111
Laurence Tate (11)	112
Luca Bangs (11)	113
Annabel Simpkins (11)	114
Liam Forsyth (12)	115
Rory Browett (12)	116
Saned Addarrat (13)	117
Jacob Robinson (11)	118
Ollie Jomar (11)	119
William Perrott (11)	120

Thomas Estley Community College, Broughton Astley

Joshua Crumpler (12)	121
Peyton Dunkley (12)	122
Imogen Buncher (13)	123
Harriet Patrick (11)	124
Poppy White (13)	125
Maisie Griffiths (12)	126
Sophie Huzmeli (12)	127
Kitty Johnston (13)	128

Wymondham College, Morley

Bethany Lansdell (11)	129
Pauline Lawrence	130
Sophia Wilson (11)	131

THE POEMS

LGBTQ Rights

LGBTQ+ is looked down upon
Just because of the person they're attracted to.
I don't think that's equal rights!
Half of the population looks down upon them.
Just because they're different, I don't think that's right.
Why do people hate the LGBTQ+ community so much?
Humanity is disgusting, this ain't right,
Just because of their attraction to someone and all because
of love,
Humanity should treat them right,
They're bullied because of it and beaten for it.
This isn't right!
The Pride parades are to show support for them
But the name-calling is not right at all,
Like queer, or even worse,
They are called sinners, weird and wrong!
Saying you will go to Hell
That's not right!
This is wrong,
They should be treated better.
Just because someone calls you that, don't let it offend you
A group of people support you
And know how you feel.
Your family and friends care about you,
You are valued, you are equal!

McKenzie Pollock (12)
Ballymoney High School, Ballymoney

Poor Things

Poor things, this is not fair!
Poor animals are being slaughtered for food.
Imagine one day you go to visit your grandma and she's gone because she was slaughtered for food!
This is how baby cows, pigs and other animals feel.
Say one day a baby cow goes to look for its mother in a field and she's gone.
Slaughtered, just so you can have dinner.
Eventually, we are going to run out,
Why can't you just eat veggies instead?
They are healthier.
Some people turn vegan where they don't eat any animal products like butter, milk, yoghurts and eggs
Or vegetarians who only eat veggies and fruit.
I understand you don't care but just try to have emotion and sympathy for these animals.
But I know some people will care which is great.
All these animals need is hope.
This is why animals are scared.
They don't feel safe anymore.

Freya Clarke (12)
Ballymoney High School, Ballymoney

My Granny Inspires Me The Most

My granny helped me tie my laces,
She helped me cycle too.
She helped me bake a cake
And we had a sleepover or two.

She let us have a sleepover with our cousins,
She let us use her hot tub and have great fun all day.
She always inspires me to do well,
She always wants me to do well.
She always loves and supports me when I do well.
She inspires me the most!
She always looked after me when I was younger,
She always kept me with joy,
We had great fun together,
I had fun playing with her toys.

My granny helped me chase my dreams,
She inspired me to become musical.
She always helped me with homework,
She always kept me right.
My granny helped me with many things,
She helped me with school and much more,
She always inspires me.
She's the one that inspires me the most!

Karis Greer (13)
Ballymoney High School, Ballymoney

It Will Be Okay

The past two years have been tough,
I honestly think everyone's had enough!
With Brexit, Covid and fires,
Lots have put on a spare tyre.

Covid's turned the world upside-down,
Lots have seemed to have a frown,
The first lockdown came
And everyone thought that was lame.

Google Classroom came along,
It made me feel confident and strong!
NHS has tried their best,
When everybody was a mess!

Staff shortages, masks and social distancing,
Really has got everyone listening,
One way systems, low supplies, empty stores,
Made people do a few more chores.

Hopefully it will come to an end soon,
I'll always be looking up to the full moon.
Covid has changed everyone's mood,
Who would ever think it could?

Lisa Fulton (12)
Ballymoney High School, Ballymoney

Environment

E   nvironment is so important so stop killing it please.

N   o one should cut down trees, they give us all our air.

V   ans and cars destroy the air so walk or cycle instead.

I   love animals but people are killing them so please stop.

R   oses are wonderful plants, but if you keep on destroying the air they will die.

O   ur food comes from the environment.

N   ow that the weather is getting warm in some places the trees are burning.

M   y family loves the environment so please stop killing it.

E   nvironment is amazing, it's wonderful.

N   ot a person should hate it, it is wonderful.

T   oday people are cutting down trees, killing animals and eating them, please stop!

Kirsty Hynds (12)

Ballymoney High School, Ballymoney

Equal

He is not her
She is not him
His voice is heard, her voice is dimmed
Pay cheques rise, pay cheques fall
"What's the difference?" says them all.

He is not her
She is not him
While he works she should cook
Table set, nothing overlooked
Everything perfect, nothing can compare
Yet he finds imperfections elsewhere.

He is not her
She is not him
He comes home with a mark on his neck
Nothing can she do or she'll get hit
He'll throw a fit and scream at her
Nothing can be done, not even the police.

He is not her
She is not him
Men rule the world, men do everything
Yet a man himself came from a woman's womb...

Sophie Wright (13)
Ballymoney High School, Ballymoney

Mum

You make me feel so bright
You bring me up when I'm down
When it's dark you show me light
You always know how to put a smile over my frown.

You care so much about me
You watched me when I first walked
You got a plaster for my sore knee
When I said my first words you heard when I talked.

You taught me to be respectful
You showed me to my first school
You told me to always be truthful
When I hurt my toe on the ground
You were there to get me into the pool.

You have been there for me my whole life
You make so many things seem fun
Thank you for everything
I love you, Mum.

Amy Nash (13)
Ballymoney High School, Ballymoney

2020-2021

Covid is here,
Deaths are up,
Masks are on,
Times are tough.

Lockdown's happening,
Pets being bought,
Everything is boring,
People being shot.

Global warming,
Polar bears being killed,
Ice caps melting,
Bear cubs being abandoned.

Different types of discrimination,
People scared in their own nation,
Online school very sad,
Even though it's not that bad.

Wars between cults,
People getting banned online,
New top YouTubers,
More and more over time.

This is what happened,
2020-2021,
Hope it gets better,
This is no fun.

Maria Gouveia (13)
Ballymoney High School, Ballymoney

Melanie Martinez

Melanie Martinez, you are such a gem
You have so many haters, but you don't listen to them
Pity Party, Playdate, Dollhouse are all a bop
I'm surprised your name isn't on top
Katy Perry, Lil Nas, Taylor Swift, who needs them
Because Melanie Martinez, your songs keep me breathing
I started listening to you when I was five
I think that's the reason I'm still alive
Your songs are great and the style of incredible
I love you so much and that's not debatable
Melanie Martinez, you are my idol
Keep writing songs and I'll hear them all
So Melanie Martinez, can we be friends?

Olivia Porterfield (12)
Ballymoney High School, Ballymoney

Future Self

Dear future me...
Are you still playing football?
Have you been scouted?
Are you in the A team?
Dear future me...
How were your GCSE results?
Did you study well?
Did you get the results you wanted?
Did you give it your best shot?
Dear future me...
Are you married?
Have you found love?
How long has it been since you met her?
Dear future me...
Are you still in contact with friends?
Have you seen them recently?
Have you lost or gained some?
Dear future me...
What job do you have?
Are you rich?
Do you live in a mansion?

Lee Steele (12)
Ballymoney High School, Ballymoney

Milo

He is the cutest ginger and white pony I have ever seen
But don't get fooled by his cute face
He is the most stubborn pony I know.
To look at him you would think butter wouldn't melt.
If he doesn't want to do something
He throws a tantrum like a toddler.
Despite all this, I love him with all my heart.

The wind in your hair makes you feel freedom.
Galloping through the woods,
Hearing the hooves on the ground.
Jumping over fences,
Feeling the partnership and passion for the sport.
Feeling the connection of love between human and horse.

Kayleigh Dean (13)
Ballymoney High School, Ballymoney

Confusing World

Growing up in this confusing world,
Not sure if I should sofa curl.
We must stay at home
And not go out the door.

"Schools are closed,"
My mum said.
"Just for the keyworkers,"
The teacher said.

Doing homework is such a job,
I have to study,
I need to work.

We need to beat this virus
To see our friends and family.
To help the hospitals
We need to stay indoors.

This confusing world
Is the norm.
We learn to queue
Because we don't have a clue!

Zack Forsythe (12)
Ballymoney High School, Ballymoney

Marshall Mathers

His dad was never there
His mum was a lifeless soul
At home he was a burden
A mere inconvenience.

His highschool sweetheart
The mother of his child
Now a ghost from his past
Every memory haunting his sleep.

"Maybe I made some mistakes
But I'm man enough to face them today."
He knows what he's done wrong
He knows he isn't perfect.

"That's why we sing for the kids
Who don't have a thing."
He grew up with nothing
So he gives his everything.

Sarah Jayne Madison (14)
Ballymoney High School, Ballymoney

You And I

I wouldn't be me without you.
You wouldn't be you without me.
Like Noah's ark going two by two.
We treat each other like royalty.
You helped me be relentless
And also be fearless.
I helped you be polite
And also to see the light.
Together we are a team
Through all times positive,
Together we make dreams.
Even when thoughts are negative
I wouldn't be me without you.
You wouldn't be you without me.
Like Noah's ark going two by two,
We treat each other like royalty.

Katrina McCurdy (13)
Ballymoney High School, Ballymoney

C Ronaldo

CR7 - Cristiano Ronaldo
Better than Lionel Messi
Joined Manchester United in the summer
The whole world was shocked.

To finisher/goalscorer with 122 goals for Man United
450 for Real Madrid
And 101 for Juventus
He's really the best, no doubt about it.

People made fun of him
When he was young
Now he's proved them all wrong.

He came from Portugal to Manchester in 2003
And joined back in 2021.

When he scored his first goal in Manchester
The crowd went crazy.

Mitchell Kirk (13)
Ballymoney High School, Ballymoney

Winter Is Calling

Winter has started and soon the snow will be falling
And after all this pollen will be calling
You will hear all the animals pitter-patter through the snow
At night the stars will be glowing
All the folk will be wrapped up well
Christmas morning you will hear the bells ringing
Phones will be pinging with Christmas wishes
No one likes taking the Christmas trees down
All the lights will be gone in the town
Spring will return with all the animals back
Most people will crack up with all the wasp attacks.

Lee Alexander (14)
Ballymoney High School, Ballymoney

A Farmer's Life

A farmer's life is hard.
They get up before the sun
And go to bed after the sun goes down.
Being a farmer is more than just a job,
It's a way of life.
Farmers are passionate about what they do,
They work through all weather conditions
To put food on our tables.
Even through Covid-19 when the world stopped
Farmers kept going to provide food for the world.
Even vegans need farmers to plant vegetables.
Without farmers there would be no Christmas dinner.
No farmers, no food, no future.

Robert Bradley (12)
Ballymoney High School, Ballymoney

Tree Lady

Tree Lady sleeps in the trees.
Comes out in the morning to feel the breeze.
Stepping in puddles higher than the sea,
Leaves falling from trees,
In the autumn breeze
Shakes coming from the distant trees.
Big trucks rise from behind the trees.
Crashing everything in their way.
Trees falling, animals running,
Smoke creating clouds.
She runs into the trees but can't escape.
All that's left is a wasteland of smoke
And tree stumps.
Where will she go?
She's got no home?

Thomas Millar (12)
Ballymoney High School, Ballymoney

Winter

It's the start of winter,
cold mornings are coming,
lots of snow and slippery roads,
everything is icy and fog is lying.

Everyone shopping for Christmas,
towns are busy,
snowmen are standing,
snowballs flying through the air,
snowflakes falling from perfectly round balls of ice.

Elderly women walk through the street,
taking pictures of everything,
drinking cups of warm tea,
watching the world go round,
thinking, *I don't have many years left!*

Jamie Boyle (14)
Ballymoney High School, Ballymoney

Winter

Winter snow glistens in the sun
Playing in it is lots of fun
You might get cold and you might get sick
Because the snow is so thick
So wrap up so you don't get cold
Go out there bare and you would be bold
Build a snowman then knock it down
But it might leave you with a frown
Slide down a hill with your sleigh
I could do that all day
Make a warm drink like chocolate or tea
Or get comfortable by the TV
Go to bed and keep warm
While listening to the winter storm.

Megan Wilson (13)
Ballymoney High School, Ballymoney

Autumn Poem

All around the landscape is turning orange and red.
The air is getting colder,
I don't want to get out of bed.
All around the leaves cover the ground,
My job is to rake them into a mound.
The air is cool, I can see fog in the air,
People going about without even a care.
Leaves falling from the trees,
The crunching under my feet.
People inside with the fire on
Munching on a bar of chocolate.
In the morning, the floor is cold,
I look outside to a blanket of gold.

Jake Logan (14)
Ballymoney High School, Ballymoney

Dad

You inspire me to work hard,
You motivate me on my way.
I never really confessed it,
I never really did say.
But, I want to tell you this
That you mean a lot,
There are many things without you
That are tough to be got.
You are the best dad,
Your love sets my soul on fire,
Unleashes my wildest of passions,
Sends me to places I've only imagined.
Allows me to be me,
I love you for that.

Jakob McVicker (13)
Ballymoney High School, Ballymoney

Fallen Brothers

Away to war we go
To greet our serious foe.
They shall take a great blow
So that our children may grow.

We will hit them with fire and will,
Our fallen brothers have not died in vain.
They will become our finest kill,
We will orchestrate their greatest pain.

Away to war we go,
On the rivers of freedom we will row.
We will show no mercy to the enemy,
Our hope is our greatest weaponry.

Jamie Christie (13)
Ballymoney High School, Ballymoney

2020

Covid-19 is serious,
It has changed our lives so much.
We all now feel anxious
About where we go and what we touch.

We've been told to stay at home
And not to leave the house.
To take one hour's exercise,
To trust the government, and not doubt.

I miss my friends and my family,
But we are staying safe and well.
We will not let this beat us,
Though at times it feels like Hell.

Sophie Davis (13)
Ballymoney High School, Ballymoney

Happy

What's wrong?
Don't be sad
Do what you like to do
Just don't be bad!

Always try your best
You can do this!
Even if it's a tricky test
Don't be negative, have confidence.

Do what makes you feel alive
Go and achieve your goals
Or learn to dive
You got this!

Do what you love
You can do anything
Be bright like a dove
Just be happy!

Anna McCandless (12)
Ballymoney High School, Ballymoney

Autumn Is A Beautiful Time

Autumn is a beautiful time.
All those leaves falling from the sky.
Every time I look up in the sky
I see all those bare trees flying high
And all those leaves swirling down from the sky.
Autumn, what a beautiful time.
Orange leaves crunch under our feet on the ground.
The leaves were not always orange,
They used to be green,
Soaring high at the top of a tree.
Autumn is a beautiful time.

Lewis Pollock (13)
Ballymoney High School, Ballymoney

We Are All Different

Gothic, cute, alt or indie,
Why does it matter how we dress?
Gay, bi, lesbian or trans,
Why does it matter who we love?
Snakes, dogs, cats or chinchillas,
Why does it matter what animal we like?
Tall, small, medium or just right,
Why does it matter how tall we are?
At the end of the day we're all human,
So how we dress, who we love,
What we like and our heights shouldn't matter.

Ellie Logan (14)
Ballymoney High School, Ballymoney

Humanity's Apology

Dear victims of BLM,
Sorry we the police are treating you differently
People think there's a difference between black and white
And that's why police aren't treating you right.

Dear Earth,
We have destroyed your forests and your oceans
We need to stop before you destroy us.

Dear animals,
Sorry we are killing you and your family
I can't change humanity.

Robert Gault (12)
Ballymoney High School, Ballymoney

My Massey Ferguson

M assey, she's very classy.

A cre upon acre she never looks back.

S ell it, no way! It's my pride and joy. When I hear the straight pipe my heart jumps for joy.

S atin red initials on the front window and a sixteen-ton Kane original trailer hooked on.

E lectric when I drive through the towns.

Y ou really should consider buying one of these tractors.

Glenn Matthews (12)

Ballymoney High School, Ballymoney

Autumn Wind

Gold and red colours all around
Leaves falling to the ground
Crunchy leaves as you walk
The air is getting colder
Now we're getting sweats on again
Watching movies near the fireplace
Swirling, twirling to the ground
A rainfall of leaves is all around
The fire crackling, children cackling
The wind swirling and whooshing.

Yasmin Archibald (14)
Ballymoney High School, Ballymoney

Marcus Rashford

Marcus Rashford,
What a kind-hearted man.
Filling stomachs and saving lives,
Plays football, missed many opportunities.
Still a hero at Manchester United,
Dealt with loads of racist abuse,
He has the skills and the mindset
To become who he wants.
Oh, Marcus Rashford,
What a legend he's going to be.

Riley Logan (14)
Ballymoney High School, Ballymoney

Winter's Night

On a dark winter's night
Snowing heavily outside
Chilling with a warm hot chocolate
A cosy fire on
Got up early and went out bright and early
Snow crunching beneath my feet
Throwing snowballs and making snowmen
The air is cold and foggy
Ice covering the windows of cars
Everyone catching a cold.

Eva Blair (14)
Ballymoney High School, Ballymoney

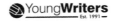

Autumn

Red and brown, the leaves fall down.
All I hear is the crunching of leaves
And the shaking of the trees.
It is so cold
And all day long the boys are bold and gold.
It is really cold, I wish I was in bed.
But instead I'm stuck outside in the cold, building a shed.
Building a shed and painting it red.

Mervyn Wilson (13)
Ballymoney High School, Ballymoney

Football

Oh, the places you will go.
There is fun to be done.
There are points to be scored.
There are games to be won
And magical things you can do with a ball.
It will make you the best winner of all.

Watching the game
Is a piece of joy
But playing the game
Is a bigger piece of joy.

Bobby Connolly (12)
Ballymoney High School, Ballymoney

Thank You

I'd like to say thank you
To the soldiers who put their lives on the line
So I can live mine.
To the soldiers that didn't eat for days
So I could.
You soldiers are the reason I can write this today.
So for your sacrifice, I'd like to say thank you.

Lewis Beech (13)
Ballymoney High School, Ballymoney

Autumn Time

Autumn is here
The leaves are orange and red
And is getting cold
People stay in their houses
Coats are being sold
The sound of leaves crunching
The leaves are falling
Water is freezing
The ground turns to ice
Autumn is here.

Lewis Henry (13)
Ballymoney High School, Ballymoney

Climate Change

While the years are slow
The weather is fast
The Earth gets warmer
As the years pass.

Further and further
Does climate change come
But climate change keeps coming
Until all is undone.

Erin Bennett (13)
Ballymoney High School, Ballymoney

Dear Friend

Friendship is the key to my heart
You never leave me apart
You comfort me when I cry
The tears start to dry.

You always keep me in your heart
You are the one who takes care of me
When no one is around me
I will never leave you apart.

We have fun together
You never leave my side
We will always have our friendship forever
You are the sunlight to my heart.

You make me happy no matter what happens
You never let me down
Our friendship is like patterns for eternity
Also like a river that flows which never ends.

My friends are my second family
Who bring sunshine when it's dark
You give me strength when I am down
All I think about is if you would ever leave me alone?

Airin Khan (14)
Joseph Leckie Academy, Walsall

True Love/Love Yourself

You were the sunlight that rose again in my life.
A reincarnation of my childhood dreams.
You were the cause of my euphoria
But, all it was was a mask full of fake emotions, fake love.

I remember what you gave me.
You gave me the courage to live.
And now you are the one who took it away.
You left me broken, unwanted.

For you, I could pretend like I was happy,
I was strong when I was hurt.
I gave the world, just for you,
I changed everything, just for you
But I don't feel love in me,
I feel like an empty shell.

All I got was an abyss garden
Full of loneliness,
This garden bloomed.
Full of thorns,
I bind myself in the darkness of my heart.

I wish love was perfect as love itself.
I wish all my weaknesses could be hidden.
I grew a flower that can't bloom; a dream that can't come
true.

My life's ruined all because of you,
Or should I say because of my naive self.
I'm so done with it, I don't want you anymore.
I just can't do it, anymore.
I'm broken from inside.

Everything you said, it's just to cover your fault.
Just cover up the truth and rip me off.

This all feels like a nightmare, that doesn't end,
This all feels like a time loop, which continues.

I want to breathe, I hate this night,
I want to wake up, I hate this dream.
I'm trapped inside an abyss, darkness; as if I'm dead.
Don't want to be lonely, save me.

It's dangerous how wrecked I am.
Save me, because I can't get a grip on myself.

So weird, at a time I for sure loved you so much.
Adapted to you with everything,
I wanted to live my life for you.
But as I keep doing that
I just can't bear the storm inside my heart.
I can't take it anymore.

I'm the one I should love in this world.
Shining the precious soul of mine.
I finally realised, so I love myself.

Not so perfect, but so beautiful.
I'm the one I should love.

I love my precious soul.
I love myself.

Mariam Lamyiah (15)
Joseph Leckie Academy, Walsall

Words Of Empowerment

Present day the pandemic rages on,
People lose hope in the shimmering of the sun,
Death tolls rise, higher than the skies,
The words of empowerment are all that get us by.

People like Rashford, doing acts of good,
Portrays the amount of his noblehood,
Being kind is what we can try,
The words of empowerment are all that get us by.

Poverty rising, food at a cost,
The rapid arrival of the snow and the frost,
Christmas nears, while Santa eats his mince pies,
The words of empowerment are all that get us by.

Celebrities, influencers, filling us with assurance,
Giving us hope, giving us tolerance,
The end of the pandemic, not anymore a lie,
The words of empowerment are what got us by.

Asad Ashraf (13)

Joseph Leckie Academy, Walsall

Friends And Friendship

Friends, we all have them.
They are like our second family.

Friends, we all have at least one friend
And sometimes our friends break our hearts
Or we break theirs
But they will always mend.

We all know the word 'friend'.
It's used all the time in our world.

Friendships, we should all have them.
They are part of our second family.

Friends, we all have them
And sometimes our friends break our hearts
Or we break theirs
But they will always mend.

We all know the word 'friend'.
It's used all the time in our world.

Friends, they make you smile,
Laugh and cry. But that's what
They're there for.

Friends, we all have friends.
Sometimes our friends break our hearts

Or we break theirs
But they will always mend.

Friends and friendship,
They are kind of the same
Friendships mean all your friends are friends
And they are in a friendship.
Friend or friends means there are one or more.

Friendships. When all your friends
'Get on'. Friendships make
You smile, laugh and cry.

Friends, we all have friends.
Sometimes our friends break our hearts
Or we break theirs
But they always mend.

You need a membership
To be in a friendship.

Friends you text
And press send.

Friends, we all have friends
Sometimes our friends break our hearts
Or we break theirs
But they always mend.

Friends and friendships
Sometimes they bring you sadness
And sometimes they bring you madness.

Friends, they are our second family.

Lola Archer (12)
Joseph Leckie Academy, Walsall

Dear My Future Self

Dear my future self,
How's it going? Hope you're good,
I hope you have achieved everything,
Got your dreams to finally come true.

Dear my future self,
Has it gone, your arch-nemesis?
Has it gone, the thing that ruined lives,
The thing that locked us away?

Dear my future self,
Is it dark, is it light?
Is it cold, is it warm?
Is it snow, is it sun?

Dear my future self,
Have you done it, completed school life?
Have you done it, got your dream job?
Has it happened, you got the best you could?

Dear my future self,
I think you got it from here.
I hope you have a good year.
So for now, goodbye.

Leah Davies (14)
Joseph Leckie Academy, Walsall

The Year 2020

The year 2020 was strange and hard for all.
Everyone was caged in their homes like zoo animals.
Education was put into the hands of a machine.
The whole world stopped like a clock that lost its batteries.
No one was going anywhere.
Fast forward several months...
Had to wear a thing called a mask unless you're a
'UAOEOMR'
Which stands for 'underage or exempt or medical reason'.
We had to wear them everywhere except home
They said a thing called 'Covid' was the criminal mastermind
for this absurd mess.
They said it could be anywhere - any town, country, city,
state, small or big, far or near, busy or not.
Nearly a year passed.
Vaccines are being tested to try and defeat this criminal.
Everyone hopes to get back to normality as lockdown fades
And #ThankyouNHS rise under all that stress, hate and
annoyance towards the lockdown and Covid-19.
Under it all I bet you a universe of wonder there is a spark of
joy, praise and delight towards it.
Maybe, just maybe if this hadn't happened
Those communities, some of the best,
Wouldn't have the support they have since Covid
Such as #blacklivesmatter and the LGBTQ+ community.
Climate change, global warming has been noticed more

And who knows, it could be solved.
I think and feel a bit good this happened.
But what are your thoughts and feelings?

Alexis Coles (13)

Joseph Leckie Academy, Walsall

Now Listen And Think

Hooray, hooray,
We're gonna be okay
At least for a while
But we'll still shout 'hooray'.

But sometimes
This isn't always the case
Someone gets hit
Maybe in the face.

The bombs are exploding
And the food is moulding
The baby is crying
Possibly dying
And while the dad is out fighting
They're barely surviving.

Now listen you monsters
Not the whole country
As some are against this
But to those who turn back to party
After that cruel attack...

Take a second to think
Before your humanity continues to shrink.

So are you really happy
With how you're destroying a country
And killing so many families?
Or is it just about the money?

And Isaac! Isaac Herzog
Stop, just stop!
You're acting crazier than a dog.

Do you even realise what you're doing?
The problems you're causing?
The people you're manipulating?
The families you're endangering
And the kids you're hurting?

But enough of those devils
I want to speak to the heroes
The ones who stay strong
And continue smiling.

Don't give up
Or lose hope
Stand with your country
I am with you
We are with you
The world is with you.

Zainab Zaakirah (13)
Joseph Leckie Academy, Walsall

Dear Mom

Thank you for trying to keep me away from the sadness
But that's all madness.

You can't protect me anymore
Because I'm growing up more and more.

I've learned the truth about life
It makes me want to sleep all the time.

Life is like a sharp knife
That pierces through the heart's cries.

Depression is the new reality
It's the only thing that stops me from being happy.

You held my hand when I was sad,
I didn't know things got this bad.

You are my mom, dad and my best friend,
I can't thank you enough,
Don't worry because I know you're there when times get
tough.

Haleema Ali (14)
Joseph Leckie Academy, Walsall

Society

Society...
Society's what makes you,
Society will change you.

It will destroy you,
Try to create a new you.

You'll look in the mirror and think,
Why am I not like the others?
But you're more than that.

It's about what lies within,
Not what sits on the surface.

How you love and care,
How you don't judge a book by its cover
And let them in, take care of them, feed them
Even when you have no other.

That's what makes you you,
Not what everyone else has to say about you.

Society shouldn't affect you.
Society doesn't make you.

Afifa Teladiya (13)
Joseph Leckie Academy, Walsall

My Poem

Others might have forgotten,
But I never can,
That the flag of my country
Furls very high,
Because of the efforts
Made by them,
My mothers, my sisters,
And those great men,
Who laid down their lives,
For a just cause,
And showed it to the world,
That Pakistan, it was!
Tears fell from the eyes
And pain rests in the heart,
Bloodshed from the bodies,
And voices across from every soul.
People didn't get weak
And they moved from what they could see,
Journeys of thousands of miles,
Got completed on a single night,
The pain was a way to gain
The nation we call Pakistan.

Laraybha Khan (12)
Joseph Leckie Academy, Walsall

Our Train To Normality (A Lockdown Experience)

The year 2020 has just begun
Everyone planning all kinds of fun
Little did anyone expect
2020 was soon to become a train wreck
March 23rd, the world came to a pause
But what was the cause?
A virus had broken out all across Earth
The name of this virus is Covid-19
Every hour felt like a day and every day felt like a week
Time dragged on as we were imprisoned in our homes
Some lost their lives, others in fear of being next
Summer has started and things are improving
We have been released from our prison cells
While our train to normality has taken off
It is not the year 2021.

Rehan Hussain (13)
Joseph Leckie Academy, Walsall

My Dear Mother

You are the key to my heart.
When I cry you comfort me with your voice.
I will do anything for you to stay with me forever.
When I was a baby you sacrificed your life for me.
Your eyes shine like a diamond ring.
Would you ever leave me?
You had many accidents, but are still happy.
You are always in my heart
And will never leave me and part.
You give me strength when I'm ill.
You are the most precious person ever.
I want to thank you for everything.
Sometimes we go through ups and downs
But no matter what,
We're always going to have a smile on our faces.

Sadia Hussain (14)
Joseph Leckie Academy, Walsall

We Are All Different

We are all different.
We all have different ways to make ourselves different.
We have a different face.
We have a different race.
We all have different hair.
Some people may find that unfair.
But what makes us who we are
Is not the way people think we are.
But what makes us unique to fight
Is all because we have human rights.
We all are different colours
Some people find that right more than others.
We all are different
From around the world
So let's be different
For the whole world to know.

Katrina Chhoker (13)
Joseph Leckie Academy, Walsall

Oppression

You gave me death, you gave me sorrow
I wish you death, or pain by torture
When I went in your domain
You killed my kind and took me away
You caged me for entertainment
You made me suffer in vain.

I wish you death, I wish you pain
I have nothing, you get all the gain.

In the day, I'm stuck in a cage
At night I'm back in chains.

This is my story, I'm a gorilla
My people loved me but now they're not here.

Ibrahim Rahman (13)
Joseph Leckie Academy, Walsall

God Is Our Only Hope

Do you know of the ancient days?
It seems like many of us do not understand,
The great and mighty power that comes from God's hand.
Where would we be without our God?
Honestly, do you think you could have made it this far?
It's like leaving a baby to fend on their own rock, our mighty stone.
Who was the one that gave Moses the power to part the Red Sea?
It seems we don't realise the power of the Lord.
He is what gives our lives more hope.

Destiny Igbinevbo (14)
Joseph Leckie Academy, Walsall

Religion - Islam

They say we're terrorists
But we know we're not
They say we drop bombs
But we know we don't.

They show us hate
We show them fate
They treat us disrespectfully
We treat them respectfully.

We believe in one God
Who is very forgiving
And many messengers
Who teach us many things.

People judge us
No matter what we do
But we are born with love
And show people in this world.

Yasmin Sidat (13)
Joseph Leckie Academy, Walsall

Labels

Another terrorist attack in the news,
But this is nothing new,
Just the media representing us wrong again.
Wait, sorry, we're to blame!
Another family seeing it happening,
They believe everything the screen is saying.
'Their religion is dangerous'...
'Oh no, I see them in the store, come and save us'...
Walk around with this label,
But how about we turn the table?

Zara Begum (14)
Joseph Leckie Academy, Walsall

Black Lives Matter

I note the obvious differences
In the human family
Some of them are serious
And some thrive in comedy.

Some declare their lives are lived
As true profundity
And others claim they really
Live the real reality.

The variety of our skin tones
Can confuse, bemuse, delight
Brown and pink and beige and purple
Tan and blue and white.

Jaxson Mohamed
Joseph Leckie Academy, Walsall

Equal Rights

The world is now a sad place
And is starting to become a disgrace.
There's always conflict and war,
And of course new laws!

Males and females should have equal rights,
But they are seen differently in people's sights.
If we help each other and work together
We can make this world better for one another.

Amina Imran (14)
Joseph Leckie Academy, Walsall

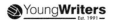

The Sea, The Sun And The Sky

Trailing across the sea,
You'll never see me.
Coming across the land,
With loads of sand.
Two people in love, gazing up at the sky,
Telling all their lies.
Forgiving their sins as the sun spins.

As crystal clear rain thrashes down in pain,
We hold each other tight,
And we remain.

Now this is us, without complaint,
Thank you to the above, you saint.

Delta Walder
The Heights Free School, Blackburn

Love Is Hard

Here we go again,
I'm in the same place as before.
This time it's different,
It's true.

It feels real, the way I feel.
I don't think she feels the same.
When I found out that she didn't feel the same,
My heart shattered into a million pieces.

Maybe one day
She will feel the same.
I will wait.

Billy Morris
The Heights Free School, Blackburn

Moment Of Madness

My head spins,
It's a crazy world.
How can I cope
When my thoughts swirl?

I feel confused,
I feel angry,
I feel scared,
Therefore I'm not repaired!

We self-destroyed
In a world that doesn't understand,
We just have to follow every command.

Megan Burns (15)
The Heights Free School, Blackburn

Roses

Roses are red
Violence is blue
If I'm pretty
Look at you.

Roses are red
Violence is blue
I'm not a single friend
Cos I got ma crew
And we stick together like glue.

Ellie Cox (13)
The Heights Free School, Blackburn

Three Versions Of Me

Dear past me,
I'm so sorry.
In all those lessons that I didn't concentrate in,
I'm sorry.
All the time I didn't try my best
And feel worked to the brim
So the water would overflow,
I'm sorry.

Dear present me,
I'm telling you something from the heart beneath.
You better put the work in
So future me can live happily.
I know you have dreams
That you want to be
And to fulfil them you have to listen to me.
But overall be yourself
And be true to me,
From future me.

Dear future me,
I hope you're living happily.
I hope you've got kids and a family.
I hope I set up a bright life for you and your family.
I hope you have a good job and are living with glee.
I hope most of all, you yourself are happy and free.

Joe Barratt
The Oratory Preparatory School, Goring Heath

What It Means To Me

When you know you can do anything
And nobody can stop you,
When you reach for the stars,
And the warm feeling inside you creeps up to your face
And you can't help but scream
And the only thing you're thinking about is reaching your
dream.

I can feel all the blood rushing through my veins
And all the crazy thoughts speeding through my brain.
I can feel a cold breeze brushing past my face
But deep down I know I can win this race.

The thrill of knowing I am enough,
Telling myself that I am tough.
The life that I know I can achieve,
The happiness that we all receive.

The weight that's lifted off my shoulders,
The fact that I'm the strongest soldier.
The fearlessness that I can see,
This is what empowerment means to me.

Kiara Kemahli (12)
The Oratory Preparatory School, Goring Heath

The World

The world is a machine
That is inspirational and great,
All you can do is wonder and dream,
However, life is not what it seems.

You go out,
To see a world of doubt,
Where everyone is without
The happiness of life,
Oh, the happiness of life.

Everyone worries
About their needs,
Putting the world at disagree,
Conflict riddles the world
Where missiles are hurled.

The countries feel dark,
Where war has made his mark,
And the world is not as happy as it seems.

But, the world is ours,
We are all empowered
To lay the seeds of something great,
To help the world be saved.

Go outside, take the world into our hands,
We're the new generation,
It's time to make our creations.

Tom Holborn (12)
The Oratory Preparatory School, Goring Heath

Make A Difference

Be who you want to be, be the person to speak out.
Be the one to change the world
Even if it only changes one thing out of one million
You might be the one to speak out in one billion.

Life isn't always fair, hope isn't always there
But you can change that.
People say nothing is impossible
But others say everything is impossible,
Those are the people you need to tell
That the word impossible says I'm possible.

So now I'm going to ask you the question,
The question I made this for,
The question I want you to say yes to
But it's your decision what the answer is.

Are you going to make a difference?

Emilia Bish (11)
The Oratory Preparatory School, Goring Heath

Fear Future Me

Dear future me,
I hope you have a family,
I hope you feel wealthy,
I hope you look healthy
And I hope you are as successful as Grammarly.

Dear past me,
I'm sorry I made you thirsty,
I'm sorry I made you murky,
I should have worked harder
Like a conqueror boxer.

Dear present me,
I want you to work as hard as you can,
I want you to get into university,
I want you to travel multiversity,
Meeting Steve Jobs and Cannavale Bobby.

Dear future me,
Remember the sun will rise
And you will always have advice,
Remember there will be back-up
And just remember never, give up.

Tiger Wang (12)
The Oratory Preparatory School, Goring Heath

Our World Is Living Too

Welcome to Earth
A beautiful place
But our world is changing
New challenges we face.

Trees are cut down
Species are dying
We must stop this
But no one is trying.

So to all the people destroying the planet
I have a couple of things to say
Here is a list of things you've done wrong
But don't worry, it'll all be okay.

We are being suffocated in a blanket of gases
And the destruction of forests and seas
Hunting animals for money
And dropping plastic in the sea.

So we should look after it
Our big world
Instead of sitting in an office
Blind to the world.

Darcy Pollard (12)
The Oratory Preparatory School, Goring Heath

Save Our Planet

The world we live in
Is a paradise within,
But every single day
Nature turns to ruin.

As we continue to be clueless
And as global warming accelerates, you are viewless.
Wildlife and species are becoming extinct,
Please stop this assassination of animals.

How would you feel
If you were treated like this?
Your home turned into an abyss,
Let's take some time to reminisce
And enjoy the beautiful outdoors.

We can save our planet,
If we put our mind to it,
We can save the animals
And stop acting like cannibals.

Please, stop destroying our planet
Because I admire it.

Archie White (12)
The Oratory Preparatory School, Goring Heath

Don't Hide In The Shadows

Self-love is an ocean,
Your heart is a vessel,
Don't get yourself caught up in a potion,
Social media is toxic,
Leading you into mazes you can't solve,
Making people dissolve.

Filters and make-up,
Leads to break-ups,
You think you're in a hall of mirrors,
With your secrets, thoughts and terrors,
All you can think of are your errors,
Don't hide
Or bottle up inside.

Self-love is an ocean
And your heart is a vessel,
Live your life and never take the knife,
Don't listen to the lies and think of the highs,
Live your life and you will get a pleasant surprise.

Amelia Cole (13)
The Oratory Preparatory School, Goring Heath

My Life

Sun shining over here,
There's a party,
Lots o' cheer,
Lots of adults having beers,
Driving around, switching gear,
Swerving away from a deer,
Steering clear,
Oh dear.

Future me, help me,
This is my sanctified plea,
Make me a cup o' tea,
There's a lock, you're the key.
Help me.

Work hard, play hard,
Don't give up, don't give in,
Whatever your challenges may be,
Set yourself free,
You can do it.

Keep healthy, keep well,
Don't cry, don't yell,
Make a mistake,
Don't dwell, ring a bell,
To tell.

Freddie Bennett (12)
The Oratory Preparatory School, Goring Heath

Be

'When the whole world is silent
Even one voice becomes powerful...'

I want to be that voice,
That light shining in the darkness.

I want to let my voice ring out,
Out of the heavens,
Out of the seas,
Out of my soul.

I want to scream from the highest mountain.
I want to sob from the deepest sea.
I want to take up arms
And have others follow me.

I want to cry, cry rivers,
Rivers of fear,
Rivers of longing,
Rivers of hope.

I want to inspire others,
And let others inspire me.

I want to be heard.
I want to be...

Iris Gray (13)
The Oratory Preparatory School, Goring Heath

Before It's Too Late

Granted is the word we take,
The lives we lead are at stake.
Once clear blue heavens now shrouded,
As the cities below are overcrowded.

Transparent oceans once teeming life,
No resources causing strife.
Once tall and verdant were the trees,
As we are the root of this disease.

You can only blame us alone,
As they say, you reap what you've sown.
This is not the end of the line,
Let us plant a new seed this time.

Preserve what we have taken for granted,
The life we have been gifted for free,
The water, skies and trees,
The life we lead needs to change.

Giorgia Fiorentino (13)
The Oratory Preparatory School, Goring Heath

Masks And Make-Up

Social media is a world,
A world of masks and make-up.
On her phone the Internet uncurled
Of stories of drama and break-ups.

With thoughts of sadness in her head
She idolises the thought of being dead.
But she needs to know that she does belong
That the life she lives can be prolonged.

She can ignore the beauty and pride
That she doesn't think she has.
She needs to only care about the beauty that's inside.

Social media is a world
It can make you feel insecure and down.
But it can also make you love this world
And the body that it surrounds.

Mallory Ross (12)
The Oratory Preparatory School, Goring Heath

Perfect

When you're scrolling through social media,
Comparing yourself to people with heaps of make-up,
A dozen filters on,
Thinking how could a person be so perfect,
When actually, no one is perfect,
Perfect isn't a word you should use
To describe yourself or anyone else.

Don't look at yourself and comment on all your flaws,
Instead, think of all the good things,
That you are and will be,
Looks don't determine a person,
They don't make you any different to the pretty girl you saw online,
Focus on yourself, no one else.

Orla Huxtable (13)
The Oratory Preparatory School, Goring Heath

Time For Change

When you think the world around you
Is looking down with greed,
Stealing your money, personality
And taking your voice from inside,
Society says you're too fat or too thin,
Or too muscular for a female body,
Steals your courage,
Your image,
Your faith in yourself and in the world.
We are women, not toys, not objects,
Or little fashion accessories you carry around.
We should not be seen as cleaners,
Or things you just take out on a date then forget.
This has gone on for too long
And it's time for things to change!

Skyla Horton-Moran (12)
The Oratory Preparatory School, Goring Heath

What Is Right?

Equality... Equality
Is this the word
The world is missing?

Why must sex and race
Decide our place?
Why must appearance control our fate?

Let us stand strong
In the place where we belong!
Let us be happy behind the face we hold,
And the past we behold!

But when those devil voices whisper,
Remember you're beautiful,
Remember you're worth it
No matter what you look like.

Those people see you through a single thought
But remember those who fought.
Fight for what's right.

Lily Bowlby (12)
The Oratory Preparatory School, Goring Heath

Ambition

Dear future me,
Help me,
Set me free
And comfort me.

I need a new life
To inspire me,
To strive and be happy!

A future of glory and pride,
Not timid and tired.
Currently, I'm stressed and pressured,
I need to start fresh and be leisured.

My strength will rise from pain,
As high as a plane.
What lies ahead
Is something I'll never dread.

I hope you do well
And if you need me, just ring my bell.
Goodbye future me,
And I hope you live joyfully!

Zubyn Mehta (12)

The Oratory Preparatory School, Goring Heath

Empower Yourself

Empower yourself
And I'll empower you,
To reach the best of your ability,
The best you can do.

Be strong, be confident,
Aim to climb higher,
Push to aspire
To be the best you can be,
Not what others want of you,
Not me, but you.

All the things that get you down in life,
Sad and distressed,
Come sit down with me,
Get some worries off your chest.

Now remember these words
And be sure that you do.
Empower yourself
And I'll empower you.

Henry Kietz (12)
The Oratory Preparatory School, Goring Heath

Beautiful

Be yourself always,
Love yourself in more ways.
Don't let others change your ways,
Put yourself in first place.

Your flaws make you beautiful,
They make you more thoughtful.
If you listen to others
They might make you cover
The real you over and over.

They'll make you lie
About the real you inside.
They'll make you shy
About the beautiful you outside.

So stand strong
And don't let others tell you wrong.
You are beautiful on and on.

Jessica Reed (12)
The Oratory Preparatory School, Goring Heath

The Mask

Knock, knock
Is there something behind this?
This layer trapping something in
It's like a mask.

Attractive but fake
If only it would smash
Then you'd be free
What are you hiding?

Natural beauty
It's as beautiful as an undiscovered island
Untouched and how it's meant to be
Our scars don't define us.

They show what we overcome
It makes us feel like someone
First impressions don't last
When you look behind the mask.

Tara Bignell (12)
The Oratory Preparatory School, Goring Heath

You

You can fly as long as you try,
You can sleep as long as you count sheep,
Once you sleep then you can dream,
Then make those dreams come true!
You can be a policeman if you please,
You can be a chef that only cooks cheese,
But remember, wherever you are,
Always still be you!
If you ride a horse and fall,
Carry on and stand tall.
If your car runs out of charge,
Try to get it to a garage.
And if in doubt, just shout,
"My dreams will come true,
And I will be me!"

Samantha Wesson (11)
The Oratory Preparatory School, Goring Heath

Life

Dear future me,
Do you have a spouse,
And live in a house?
I hope you have friends
And don't live in the ends.

Dear future me,
Don't dawdle,
Be affordable,
Use your money well,
Don't dwell on your problems,
Learn from them

Dear future me,
You will have a great life,
You'll get a wife,
You'll be happy
Because life ain't crappy.

Now, when you're happy
Future me,
Smile with glee because you're happy.

Thomas Eady (12)
The Oratory Preparatory School, Goring Heath

What Inspires Me?

There are many things that inspire me;
My teachers, my friends and my family.
My idols who live happily
But my dad inspires me the most.

His head that never gives up,
His words build up our trust.
His hands to work he must,
My dad inspires me the most.

His legs that never stop moving,
His smile that keeps me uplifted,
His heart that is constantly beating,
Dad, you inspire me the most.

Make sure to have someone who inspires you
As my dad inspires me.

Noah Moore (12)
The Oratory Preparatory School, Goring Heath

Lift Your Life

Dear future me,
I am living happily,
Spread your wings like a bird,
And grow strength like a tree.
Don't keep to your sorrows, just focus on glee.
Don't keep to your lies, just think truthfully.

Life is a gift,
Don't slow it down, just keep it swift.
Keep it steady, don't let it shift.
Let yourself loose, don't keep yourself stiff.
Life is a river, don't keep it still, let it drift.
Don't stick to the ground, let your life lift.

Jasper Vaughan (13)
The Oratory Preparatory School, Goring Heath

Let Them Be

Dear future me,
I hope you're happy
Married with kids and a family
Give them the key
To set them free.

The injustice
Prejudice
Please let them aspire
To be something higher
Than a middle-class citizen
In a bad situation.

Don't let them forget their ancestry
Teach them to do things differently
No one's normal
We're all abnormal
Please see them through
In what they want to do.

Dylan Wheat (13)
The Oratory Preparatory School, Goring Heath

Who Are You?

You can be anything,
So who are you?
Will you be the person who speaks their mind?
Will you be the person who is very kind?
Will you be the person who looks after sheep?

Will you choose to be silent or shout?
Will you live in happiness or doubt?
Will you choose to love or to hate?
Will you be early or late?

Would you give up or persevere?
Anything, anyone,
Who are you?
And who do you want to be?

Mia Burridge (11)
The Oratory Preparatory School, Goring Heath

Women

We're powerful,
We're strong.
Some people take us as a joke,
Some people take us for granted,
Some people think we are objects.
For years men have looked down on us
As cleaners, maids and housewives, until now.
They think it's okay to catcall us on the street
As we walk past, scared to walk home at night.
Women are not objects,
Women are powerful.
Women are strong.
Don't tell me I'm wrong!

Scarlett Baker (12)
The Oratory Preparatory School, Goring Heath

Global Warming

Polar bears are dying,
Antarctica is trying
To fight the mess we made
And we're staying the same
We're the cause of global warming
Show some love and start supporting
Koalas are hiding
As their forest home is passing
Ocean life is disappearing as plastics
Their new home
The world revolves around social media
Go outside, make a change
If we stop plastic
The world could be fantastic.

Emily Caine (11)
The Oratory Preparatory School, Goring Heath

Reality

You are worth it,
You are strong,
Don't quit
Because you do belong.

Don't back away
Because you're enough,
And your future awaits
Even when it gets rough.

You see people, through a lens,
And bits of their life
But that's not reality,
It's all just design.

You need to dig deeper,
Not just your cover,
But what's beneath
Will recover.

Dorcus Hobley (12)
The Oratory Preparatory School, Goring Heath

Climate Crisis

We are killing the Earth
And no one is crying,
Little do we know but the world is dying.
The Arctic is fading and the polar bears are going,
But where do they go?
We have melted their home.
Go on a bus, not in a car,
Before everything's been taken
And we've gone too far.
Throw away your plastic,
Don't leave it hanging,
Before it's too late
And you'll be drowning.

Amy Prodhan (11)
The Oratory Preparatory School, Goring Heath

Peace Perfect Peace

Magic, magic wand
What would I wish for?
A million dollars
Or peace.
Peace in countries,
Peace with your family,
Peace with your friends
And once you're at the top
Reach out your hand
And preach peace, hope and joy.
Because you are only as loud and strong
As you tell yourself - so remember this -
Why don't you take one more step
And see where it gets you...

Freddie Sallis (11)
The Oratory Preparatory School, Goring Heath

Heard

Know there is somewhere to go,
If you are turning to and fro,
Somebody will be there,
If you are in despair,
There will be an open door,
If you ever need one for
Anything bad you come across,
That makes you feel lost.
So please make your voice heard
If you ever feel alone,
And know you are not alone in finding your voice,
So push through it,
Do not be ashamed to admit.

Kitty Thomas (11)
The Oratory Preparatory School, Goring Heath

Believe

You!
Yes, you!
You, be you!
You, do you...?

If you believe anything is possible.
If you try anything is possible.
If you enjoy anything is possible.

'Can't' is only a word,
You can stay away
Or not be heard,
Even fly like a bird,
But if for only a second, one moment
You believe you can't,
Then you're not gonna be a happy man.

Finley South (12)
The Oratory Preparatory School, Goring Heath

I Am Glad To Be Me

When I look at me
All I see is me
And nobody else can quiz me
But many will miss me.

I am so special
And that's what it seems
From my head to my feet
That's what I find so sweet.

My size, my shape
That is me, there is no one else I would rather be
My skills, my pride, my outside is just fine
And all of that makes me glad to be me!

Harry Wakeman (12)
The Oratory Preparatory School, Goring Heath

Girls Can!

You can't do it because you're a girl.
We get told we're either too fat or too thin.
There is nothing to do ever to make us win.
It's always boys can do this but girls can't do that.
You need more make-up, you're not pretty.
Don't do that because you're a girl.
This is your chance to prove them wrong
And this is your chance to be strong!

Anya Jacobs (12)
The Oratory Preparatory School, Goring Heath

Empower

Raise your voice, speak up,
Make yourself heard,
Speak your mind.

Speak for others,
Speak for yourself.

Talk to people,
Talk to them and empower them.

Reach up.
Reach for the stars
And do your best.

Take part in projects.
Take what you are given.
Pick it up and make it gold.
Good luck in the future.

Finn Mackenzie (12)
The Oratory Preparatory School, Goring Heath

Feel Happy

Don't be sad
Don't be bad
Don't be mad
Because all you're doing is hurting you
You could even hurt others too.

So stand up and deal with that thing
That makes you feel like such an unhappy being.

And fight
For what's right
And start your day feeling happy
Start your day feeling... like me!

Ronnie Phares (12)
The Oratory Preparatory School, Goring Heath

Our World

Just remember
To care for our environment
And preach
Because your voice is empowerment.

The world is our home
The planet is our place
Walk with confidence
Always with a smile on your face.

We need to save this world
And get off your phone
Stop looking at your screen
But make trees fully grown.

Barnaby Badcock (13)
The Oratory Preparatory School, Goring Heath

What's In The Future?

Dear future me,
I ask you
To follow your hopes and dreams,
If things go bad,
You will get mad,
But don't give up
And push yourself back up.

Dear future me,
I ask you
To look in the ocean
And see all the commotion
That is going on under the waves,
At all of the fishes' graves.

Rosie Davis (12)
The Oratory Preparatory School, Goring Heath

Dear Future Me

Dear future me
All I ask is be happy
When days are grey
Don't be sad
Don't get mad
When you're mean, think
What have I seen?
Where have I been?
Have hope in me
Dear future me
Help me see
That together we can be happy
And save the planet
And be thankful we still have it.

George Hall (11)
The Oratory Preparatory School, Goring Heath

Alive

I am nature,
You are nature,
We are nature,
Everything is nature.
We grow trees and live on the bees' knees,
We care for animals and love malls
Where we can look at the moles.
Some creatures grab fruit with their feet
While others scavenge for meat.
We are alive,
This is life...

Lucas Teixeira (12)
The Oratory Preparatory School, Goring Heath

Sea

Fear future me,
Don't throw stuff in the sea.
Have faith in me, please trust me.
Let people see that you don't put stuff in the sea.
We can do so much more,
It is time to explore
And make it all clean.
If we stick together
We will make the world better.

Toby Jomar (12)
The Oratory Preparatory School, Goring Heath

Women - Empowerment

We are called women,
Not things,
Not victims,
Not maids,
Not slaves,
We fought for our rights,
To be able to be leaders,
To vote and to have voices.
We want to go out at night,
To walk home alone,
We are humans,
We are called women.

Erin Robertson (11)
The Oratory Preparatory School, Goring Heath

If There Were None

If there was no water,
There would be no life,
No humans, no animals.

If there were no life
There would be no fun,
No people to talk to.

So let's save our planet
And make the world the best,
Let's keep the world at rest.

Freddie Bowlby (11)
The Oratory Preparatory School, Goring Heath

Family

Family is special to me.
They will always be there for me.
We have ups and downs
But they will always help.
I love them and they love me.
Family, family, we help each other
Through the good and the bad.
Our love is endless like the void of space.

Laurence Tate (11)

The Oratory Preparatory School, Goring Heath

You Can Be Great

Dear future me,
Have hope in me,
Please let them see how great I can be.
If they don't I shall still succeed
To show everybody just what they can be
And when they do we can all be a team
To save our planet
And so everybody can be pleased.

Luca Bangs (11)
The Oratory Preparatory School, Goring Heath

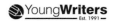

Spelingz

Y iz everyting sew hrd too spel?
I cnt doo enyting probaly.
I woz alwys botom off speling tezts.
I cn nt spel.
Tiz sew :-(

I wesh tht I coud gust mack ep anyting
Amd peple woud no wat I sed.
Y iz speling sew hrd?

Annabel Simpkins (11)
The Oratory Preparatory School, Goring Heath

Don't Stop

If you achieve something don't stop
Keep on going till you make it to the top
When you make it, take a break
Then reward yourself with some steak
Wake up and lie in bed
Then spread kindness till you're dead!

Liam Forsyth (12)
The Oratory Preparatory School, Goring Heath

Live Life

Life is a gift,
Exercise is the lift.
A healthy body will energise,
A full life will realise.
So take the time
And move into your prime.
So make it last,
Live life for the future not the past.

Rory Browett (12)
The Oratory Preparatory School, Goring Heath

Football

Football is the beautiful game
It makes everyone happy
It brings us together all around the world,
From England to Brazil,
Germany to Japan.
We don't need to fight
When football can unite.

Saned Addarrat (13)
The Oratory Preparatory School, Goring Heath

What We Can Be

To future me,
Have faith in me.
Help them to see
What we can be.
If we work together
We can make the world better
In stopping them from
Draining the life from the sea.

Jacob Robinson (11)
The Oratory Preparatory School, Goring Heath

Dear Future Me

Dear future me
Make sure I never drink tea
Make sure I never litter in the sea
And make me never eat peas
Plus, make me not be stung by a bee
Don't let my life ruin me.

Ollie Jomar (11)
The Oratory Preparatory School, Goring Heath

Be Yourself

You are amazing at being yourself.
You are terrible at being other people.
Do not change because others change around you.
Be yourself because everyone else is taken.

William Perrott (11)
The Oratory Preparatory School, Goring Heath

Words Hurt

I woke up in the morning feeling tired,
I had to get up and make my students inspired.
I listened to my students' ideas
But they don't listen to each other,
It brings tears to my eyes.
When I watch them cry they look up to their famous football player
or their favourite basketball player.

They play with each other but leave another out
Abandoning them in the darkness with their sadness
And don't know what to do, they're stuck in an abyss
But the others don't realise they're just playing,
Like nothing is wrong,
They're not ready for the real world,
They might finally understand the words they say
Aren't just a joke or a laugh
But they're memories that people will have.
They'll remember you as that kid, the one that is a bully,
The mean one, the bad one, but they don't know what they did.
The person is hurt inside but on the outside they're happy
But inside they're really sad.

Joshua Crumpler (12)
Thomas Estley Community College, Broughton Astley

Empower

'I love you' can make you feel safe
But it can also be fake.
Little white lies are hiding behind the prettiest of eyes
And it's crossing the line to say you're just fine when you're not.
You need to smile and ignore the vile and sarky comments people say at school.
Just don't fall into the rabbit hole of the roles into which you don't follow.
Just say 'I wanna be me', who you really are
Not who they want you to be,
Love who you are,
Yes, you're different,
And that's what we want them to see.
Don't go too far,
Just let them see who you really are.
Stand for it, don't take their hits.
They're just rude, ignore the comments that are crude
Love yourself and accept yourself,
Before you fade away.
Everyone would cry if you learned to fly
So stay, for at least another day.

Peyton Dunkley (12)
Thomas Estley Community College, Broughton Astley

My Future Self

M y future self,
Y ou need to remember what you used to do.

F loat in the pool and try not to sink.
U nder your bed you thought that there was a monster.
T uck yourself under a blanket and scare your parents.
U ndergoing a meltdown in a public place.
R eading always had to be a bore.
E ating food was only fun when it sounded like a plane.

S leeping was the last thing that you wanted to do.
E lf on the Shelf was so exciting every morning of December.
L oneliness was not a word in your vocabulary.
F orgetting these things would be bad because you loved them.

Imogen Buncher (13)
Thomas Estley Community College, Broughton Astley

Dear Future

Don't ever fall so far from this place,
Into so much self-doubt and hate.
Always try to keep a positive face,
Because life can be great!

Don't ever get to the point where you become too
damaged,
Remember there are people that value and love you.
If you feel you cannot manage
Turn to your family and friends
Because their love will always be true!

Do everything in your power to find a happy place,
Things are bound to get better soon.
Always give yourself time and space,
Set your goals high and reach for the moon.

Harriet Patrick (11)
Thomas Estley Community College, Broughton Astley

When I'm Older...

When I'm older
I want to make everyone proud.
I want to get my dream job.
I want to be happy.
I want to think about others, not just myself.
I want to inspire, to make others happy.
I want to change lives.
I want to be me.

I don't want to be rich.
I don't want a fancy house.
I don't want an expensive car.
I just want to be me.

I just want an ordinary house.
I just want an ordinary car.
I just want to help and inspire, and to love.
I want to be me.

Poppy White (13)
Thomas Estley Community College, Broughton Astley

Family

Family, can they ever go away?
Can they ever escape your day?
No, they cannot,
Which I am thankful for.
They pick me up when times are rough,
Even though getting along with them is tough
I wouldn't trade them for any other family
Because they are my world,
I am so thankful for them
And would do anything to help them.

Maisie Griffiths (12)
Thomas Estley Community College, Broughton Astley

Family

F amily is family no matter how far apart.

A lways remember that they are close at heart.

M any people see relatives every day.

I n some families, people live far away.

L ots of people miss their family and keep in touch by phone.

Y ou need to know, that you are not alone.

Sophie Huzmeli (12)

Thomas Estley Community College, Broughton Astley

If I Could Have One Wish

If I had one wish,
I might say to have world peace.

If I had one wish,
I might say to end world hunger.

If I had one wish,
I might say to end all crimes.

Some might say
A hat, a bag, a plane,
But I'd say peace.

Kitty Johnston (13)
Thomas Estley Community College, Broughton Astley

Animal Cruelty

Animals are suffocating and dying
We humans are killing and lying
Humans do things their own way
While animals have to be slaughtered and pay
Elephant tusks are on display
Their herd when one is gone are in dismay
Tigers are made for living room rugs
Animals' lives have been taken for drugs
Stag heads are on the stone walls
Animals being killed and hearing their lonely calls
Ladies wearing fur coats
Animals being sent away on boats
Puppy farms are overflowing
While rare animals are lowing
Something has got to be done
We won't stop until we've won.

Bethany Lansdell (11)
Wymondham College, Morley

Powerful Rise

Superior gender: girls versus boys
Does this really excuse them using us as toys?
'It was just a joke' and 'we're just having fun'
All I want to do is pull out a gun.

You do the cleaning! You do the cooking!
Maybe I should just poison the man
I'd enjoy watching the choking!

Why is it that because we're different
We don't have equal rights?
We take the work while men only have frights.
So, come on, rights for women!
Or are you just scared we're more powerful than given.

Pauline Lawrence
Wymondham College, Morley

Mirror Mirror

When I look in the mirror,
I see a woman who is...
Powerful,
Unique,
Fearless,
Brave
And beautiful.

When I walk down the street,
I see women who are...
Confident,
Strong,
Unstoppable,
Remarkable
And amazing.

When I listen to music,
I hear about women who are...
Vocal,
Smart,
Iconic,
Determined
And heroic.

All women are superheroes,
Including you.

Sophia Wilson (11)
Wymondham College, Morley

YOUNG WRITERS INFORMATION

We hope you have enjoyed reading this book – and that you will continue to in the coming years.

If you're the parent or family member of an enthusiastic poet or story writer, do visit our website **www.youngwriters.co.uk/subscribe** and sign up to receive news, competitions, writing challenges and tips, activities and much, much more! There's lots to keep budding writers motivated!

If you would like to order further copies of this book, or any of our other titles, then please give us a call or order via your online account.

Young Writers
Remus House
Coltsfoot Drive
Peterborough
PE2 9BF
(01733) 890066
info@youngwriters.co.uk

Join in the conversation!
Tips, news, giveaways and much more!

 YoungWritersUK 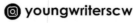 YoungWritersCW youngwriterscw